Hogan How Two: Ben Hogan's Five Lessons Distilled

by K. Zachary Haslem

Acknowledgments

This short list of people who have influenced my golf game in paternal ways excludes the golfers who impressed me with their games and instruction, without knowing who I was. That list includes Ben Hogan, Annika Sörenstam, David Duval, Sir Nick Faldo, Butch Harmon, Larry Nelson, Tiger Woods, David Leadbetter, Tom Lehman, Fred Couples, Phil Mickelson, and Corey Pavin. I may have left some out. I'll remember later. They are the people from my impressionable period. The time in a golfer's life when they are becoming inspired. Currently, I'm inspired by Collin Morikawa and Jon Rahm.

The people I've known, who are no less influential, are the ones I actually acknowledge with credit for making this book a reality. My Dad, Rick Haslem, who instilled the values and love of the game that has carried me through long after others would have quit. My late brother, Harley Haslem, for being all the things only a brother can be. Not least of which was my first golfing partner.

PGA Professional Joe Cullinane Jr., for giving me the best first job a boy can have. Picking the range at night, in exchange for an hourly wage and a bucket of balls, per day. Plus permission to pick that bucket up and hit it as many times as I wanted. The clubs I played during those six years with Joe as my pro are so worn the stickers on the shafts have gone long past legible. They're practically embedded into the metal. Had things turned out differently, our six years would have extended into something greater.

More recently, Brian Logsdon and Rob Little. Brian for acknowledging that golf was central to me. In large ways only Brian could make look small. Rob for sharing a burning desire within himself, he'd always eluded to, in such a way as to inspire myself and others.

These are my paternal influences. May we all have them, in golf and in life.

"One look is worth a thousand words," also phrased as "a picture is worth a thousand words."

If a single picture is worth a thousand words, the compendium of images collected into a whole, found throughout Ben Hogan's Five Lessons: The Modern Fundamentals of Golf must be worth exponentially more.

"Sports are 90% inspiration and 10% perspiration."
Johnny Miller

Preface

I count the greatest shot I ever hit, not for where it landed, but for where it flew. For one moment in time the ball rose above the moon, so full and blue in the Nevada sky. It floated above the crisp upper rim. All else was dark save but for my target orb, and I would be exiting over the fence as I had many times before. For no golf pro, no matter their patience, could wait till I had my fill of the game.

A keer is a time or a turn in Dutch. My first name keern is a dialectic variation on the Dutch word, which means to turn on time. Turning on time is the thing good golfers do best. Golfing icon and multiple major winner William Ben Hogan figured out why the turn was so instrumental to a good golf swing and how to release the club correctly. He got so good at timing his turn and releasing the club correctly, they say he would play out of the same divot all four days of a golf tournament.

Table of Contents

Prologue

In my previous book, *Hogan How To*, I outlined the hurdles a golfer would need to overcome, to wrap their mind around the differences between Hogan's methods and the standard approach. I realized, as fall progressed (*Hogan How To* was published the first week of October) those readers would have much to go on. And the road I was traveling could only enlighten them further. Readers of *Hogan How To* learned how to use a rehearsal motion. The secrets arrived at in *Hogan How To* were derived from new information in Chapter 5, that was then assimilated through the book, back to the beginning. In context of my own growth, I began the year ready to build a new swing, with the electrified action from Chapter 1 as my end goal. In August and September the benefits came to fruition. I had cut almost five whole shots off of my handicap and started to sniff rounds in the sixties. Then I realized an important next step. I was playing with a friend and my scores slipped a bit. (Due in part to the unattended fall greens). The content of *Hogan How To* stuck with me. And I realized "I could lose it all," wasn't such a bad thing. Ian Baker Finch still loves the game, even though he hasn't played at a top level for decades. So, I completely relinquished the given we all consider tantamount.

A major clue to that next step was given in the final chapter of *Hogan How To*. We saw Hogan, in his classic finish position, and two targets. One for the ball and one for his hips. We'd already explored the validity of the line extending from our front foot. So I was left wondering, just how much emphasis should be placed, down the line, on the ball target? First, I tested this notion with my practice club simulator. Years ago, Tom Bertrand issued videos describing Hogan practice methods with a cut down five iron. He intended for people to practice in slow motion. I wasn't sure that sounded necessary, but his admonition of working with a practice club has merits. When we permit ourselves to forget the ball we create swing possibilities that couldn't otherwise exist.

On the simulator, I saw incredible consistency. The aspect I see, especially in good players, is the ability to manipulate the club at the bottom. This can be an asset, or it can be a detriment. For instance, during a good round a difficult shot is required. (Imagine a shot that contends with a hazard). There are multiple things going through the golfer's brain. To avoid the hazard, and continue the series of good shots, the golfer must eliminate negative thoughts. That is hard to do when every swing has relied on correct face manipulation. Entirely too often, players who could be standouts permit their hands to bail at these times. The very strength that makes them good also makes them capable of choosing safety over excellence.

What happens when the swing is given a definitive intention, other than manipulating the club face?

Every step along the way, I've deferred to Five Lessons. For years I'd been stumped by the instruction. As time has gone by, elements of Five Lessons have become clearer. I've had to ingrain them, to make them clear. This book is about Getting over the curve that constitutes disbelief, and to the downhill traverse that is continual growth.

As with *Hogan How To*, illustrations which overlay various information from *Five Lessons* will be shown. The original illustrations will be cited by page number. Please thumb through your copy of *Five Lessons* to the illustrations being referenced.

What did I have to lose? When I asked myself, "what next?" You may recall the question, "what next?" As we left off from *Hogan How To*.At the time, I felt the what next was simply the Hogan waggle. I was correct. *Five Lessons* lead me an unexpected place though. To a complete abandonment of the given, that holds almost all golfers—from seasoned touring professional, to rank amateur— back. Beyond the back-cover-to-front-cover directive we learned to explore in *Hogan How To*within*Five Lessons* is an obvious, (in retrospect) aspect of Hogan's swing, and instruction, that dotted lines describe.

Connecting The Dots: Ben Hogan's Five Lessons Distilled examines the interconnectedness of the dotted lines in Anthony Ravielli's illustrations. *Five Lessons Distilled* is a drink with complexity, spirits meant to be aged, in true purist fashion.

Chapter 1

Correct v Incorrect Information

In *Hogan How To: Ben Hogan's Five Lessons Distilled* we took previous readers of *Ben Hogan's Five Lessons: The Modern Fundamentals of Golf* through a revisitation of the book, beginning with the new information from the fifth, Summary Chapter, back to the beginning of the book. In that process, a more perfect approach to replicating Mr. Hogan's swing was given.

In *Hogan How 2: Ben Hogan's Five Lessons Distilled*, we follow a course from A to B, through the illustrations Anthony Ravielli did for *Ben Hogan's Five Lessons: The Modern Fundamentals of Golf*. The clues are every bit as overt as those found for *Hogan How To*, except they flow from the beginning of the book to the end.

These chapters will converge in *Chapter 4: Connecting The Dots* The very first dots to connect are found on page 26. There we find dotted lines parallel to solid lines, describing correct vs. incorrect grip position, through the "trail" hand. Believe it or not, the illustrations of *Five Lessons* are so rich, an entire swing can be built on the dotted lines alone. As they are seen there, in comparison with the alternative.

On the same page, we see bold dotted lines culminating in an arrow. That arrow stems from the pinch point between the thumb and hand of the lead hand. This pinch point gets more exaggerated in experienced golfers.

Practicing and playing golf is a process of developing muscles and flexibility, in the right parts of the body. Progress is not merely the result of knowledge or luck, the most prominent differences — in a golfer's physique — can be found in their lead arm. Slicers take note. The muscle between the thumb and palm of a seasoned golfer's lead hand is **thick**, thicker than a porterhouse steak.

For reference of this phenomenon, turn to page 102, in *Five Lessons*. Seen there is the rolling motion of the lead hand past impact, to the bottom of the swing. In Ravielli's shading of the lead hand, the muscle between the thumb and hand is noticeably raised. In contemplating this motion, how do you suppose the hand would develop such a muscle?

Pulling the club through, with that lead hand, emulating the bowed wrist and rolling action, there is a distinct sensation of flexion to the crown of that muscle. The thumb is working against being bent backward. It becomes the utmost lead point of the motion, through the bottom of the swing. [1]

---

[1] The bottom of the swing is not the ball. Hogan went to great lengths to simultaneously reveal and conceal the true bottom of the swing. Which will be demonstrated through connecting the dotted lines in *Five Lessons*

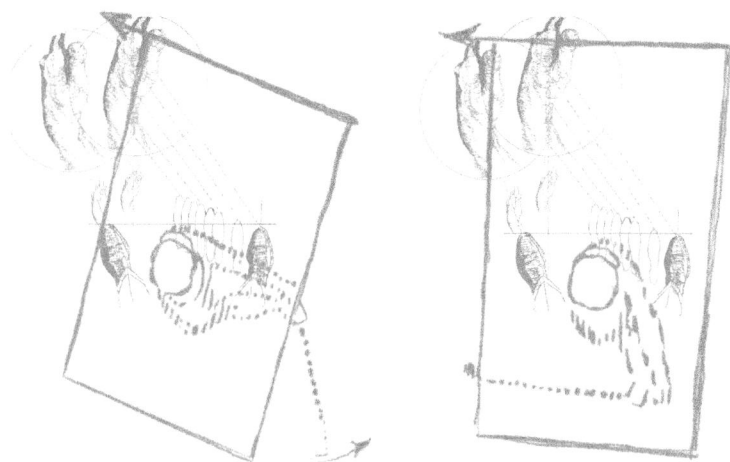

Images overlayed from page 42 (front foot quarter turn), 89 (plane), 102 (supination), and 125 (stance)

What does that muscle do? It prevents the raising of the club. It keeps the club in position between the thumb and the hand. Slicers, there is a notable breakdown of the relationship between the club, and the lead (left hand) palm, in your swing faults.

Not only do slicers benefit from this knowledge, though. A golfer must experience an outpacing of the thumb from the club, to experience the full escalation of the Hogan swing. Hogan described his motion as keeping the club face square to the target throughout the through swing, from ball to finish, he held the club face in a true position. This requires a deftness of motion, that amounts to mentally outpacing the fastest moving object in the golf swing: the club.

A crucial element of note is the center of the swing. Shown in the previous image by the intersection of lines ahead of the lead toe, and from the lead heel to the ball. That intersection governs a great many things in the golf swing.

On page 29, our next dotted line, a thick one, indicates the correct position of the "trail" hand, on the golf club. Unlike the lead hand, which is laid upon the club to lead through to that raised thumb muscle, the "trail" hand is positioned to align squarely with the target.[2]

We experience this, at address, and note that a similar strengthening of the thumb to palm muscle occurs, as a result of practice. As with the lead hand, the dominant hand experiences a rising of the club, through the bottom of the swing, which must be managed. The act of managing that rise builds that muscle.

Failure to build that muscle is due to wrong thinking. From the top of the swing, the golfer's mission is not to cause the club to descend on the ball. Doing so will make the club, "hit the back of it." As Mr. Hogan said in his famous lesson on starting the downswing with the hips. link

In *Hogan How To*, golfers learned a rehearsal motion based upon a simple principle. From the top of the back waggle, the club head will descend on the ball only if the club face is allowed to pass square. As per Hogan, consistent, quality golf shots are arrived at by keeping the club face in sync with the body through to the finish. The descent of the club head, onto

---

[2] The word trail is in quotations because the widely accepted reference to the dominant hand is trail hand. Even though Hogan's use of the trail hand is anything but.

the ball, will occur through correct body motion. The surest way to implement correct body motion is in rehearsal. Maybe two percent of golfers can satisfy correct motion from address position, without rehearsal. However, understanding the dynamic action from the illustrations in this book will be a huge help—to both that 2%—and the remainder of the golfing world.

Tying The Lead to The Release

In the gravity-driven descent of the club, the position of the hands dictate the club will swing out and above the ball. That position occurs, in the second stage of the rehearsal motion because the club face is not permitted to close past square. The most recent dotted line we noted, on page 29, pointed upward from the dominant hand toward the chin, at address.

We've also visited page 102, where we see a dotted line going downward, from the lead hand to what we suppose would be the ball. Except, the caption reads, "the left wrist begins to supinate at impact." We can all see the left wrist *began to supinate* a step earlier than the dotted line. This is important, because of the location of the bottom of the swing.

The true bottom of the swing coincides with the dotted line on page 41. Located inside the instep of the left foot. The degree of supination shown on page 102 is consistent with the position of the hands as they pass that line. For proof, simply compare the drawing of Hogan on page 103, at impact, with the supination positions from 102. The lead wrist is bowed the same as the position before the dotted line.

Hogan's greatest swing speed was the bottom of the swing. At impact, his intentions were beyond impact, to the bottom of the swing. The ball merely got in the way. This overlay illustrates how the dotted line from the supination images coincide with the lead line. In the previous chapter, we saw how Hogan measured this position, and created a repeatable aim point, beyond which the ball and his swing would diverge.

The supination at the dotted line, on page 102, lined up with the dotted line from page 41 demonstrates just how far Hogan expected to turn leading into impact.

Hogan's advice on the positioning of the lead foot appears to be obsequious. That is, until we assemble the image from page 42 with the others. There are three principle drawings, which must be explored. First, the image from page 42 depicts, in exacting detail, what is meant by a quarter turn. A full turn being 90 degrees from perpendicular to the target line, and a half turn being 45. A quarter turn, then falling in-between.

A simple page turn gives us a view from above, as the hips and shoulders turn to positions relative to the quarter turned front foot. The image from page 45, from above, conjoined with the stance image from page 125—of a golfer's point of view—more broadly demonstrates how the geometry of the swing is built from the ground up.

First, we see how the stance coincides with the lines created by the shoulder turn and hip turn.

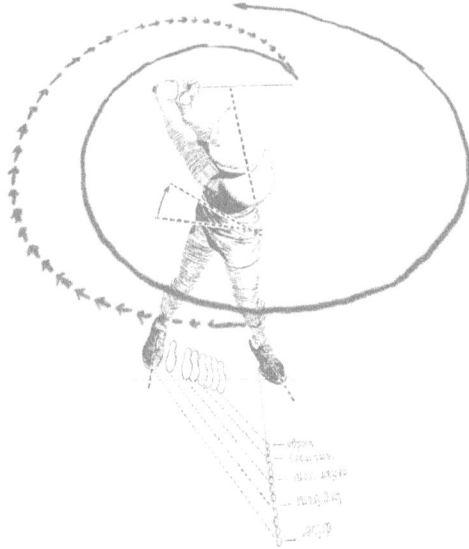

Pages 45, 103, (the correct arc) and 125 conjoined,
demonstrate the action that is about to occur, from the top of
the backswing.

Viewing the above image reminds me of a YouTuber with
many fascinating takes on the golf swing. One of which being,
swinging the club from a midpoint in the shaft. If you haven't
already, I recommend visiting Overhand Golf/The Holy
Grail. His work since Hogan's Angle was uncovered has done
a great deal to expand golfer's understanding.

If we take this combination of drawings one step further, to
one taken in *Hogan How To*, we align the center point of the
stance diagram with the lead foot. In doing so, we see two
things. How the weight is first pressed into the ball of the
front foot. And also how the weight of the body is compelled
to transfer back, to behind the golfer. We see this second

weight transfer in the new position of the footprint behind the lead leg.

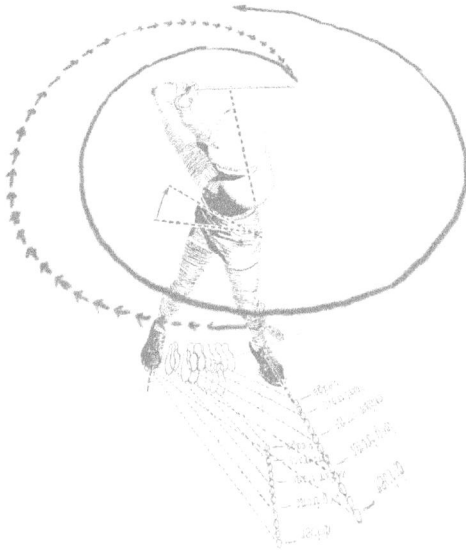

The positions seen here are famously noted as Hogan's pivot, and extraordinary leg action. As they occurred over the lead foot.

One objection a savvy golfer may have, is to the position of the ball, after impact. Noting that the club head would be moving inward, across the ball, after impact. Not only is this true, it is also ideal. Hogan came from the inside. As the correct downswing arc demonstrates. Then returned to the inside. Along with his weight. Take note of the arrow at the top of the through swing arc. That tidbit coincides with the weight shift to the aft. To the new location of the footprint.

The motions we have covered so far in this chapter are prominently lead leg and lead arm driven. Except for the arc. The next question is, how does the dominant hand and arm contribute to the release?

Let us begin first with the connection of the hips and body to the arms. From there, we can see how initiating the downswing with the hips puts the dominant arm into position to fire. The following sequence overlays the images from pages 94 and 95, which show an imaginary tether connecting Hogan's hips to his hands, at the wrist, with the images from page 91. Which demonstrate Hogan's example of a heavy rubber band pulling the hips to a wall behind the golfer. When linked together, we see how the inauguration of the swing with the hips initiates a lowering of the hands into firing position.

I'm annoyed when I see instruction that calls upon the golfer to back themselves up to a wall, and swing. For the simple fact that the hips must move backward, away from the ball. As we saw in the stance/swing diagram. That weight shift is one of the prevailing differences between a good golf swing and a bad one. Hogan depicted the distance between the golfer and the wall.

The term "hitting the wall" is in itself a misnomer. As hitting the wall is a form of negative reinforcement. No intelligent person wishes to hit a wall. Similarly, backing all the way up to the wall, at address, is a good way to experience push back against the correct motion. Hogan knew better. And yet, this is just one of many examples of how neglected his instruction has become.

Chapter 2

Feel Is Not Real?

Even good players struggle to connect their hip action with their hand action. They know, like all of us, that the hips must flash hard laterally and turn. The act of putting the club to the ball is somehow so often separate, though. That is why so few golfers have mastered the one shape shot. And those who do score better.

The difference between what we find when we delve deeply into *Five Lessons*, and what we've come to know as standard instruction, is a matter of perspective. Mr. Hogan had in mind what must occur from within the golfer. The vast majority of instruction—that fails to understand him—stems from stills and videos of the golf swing, as seen from the outside. Arguments against *Five Lessons* abound on the subject of feel vs. real. The arguer wants the freeze-frame imagery to uphold their standard. A true disciple of Mr. Hogan's, will pursue the feels, with utmost contentment.

Hogan swing sequence from 122 and 123 overlayed in temporal time. That is how we recollect the feel of a good shot.

The hallmark of a good golfer who struggles with shot shape is "on days." Some days are superb. The timing is just there. An unconscious connection of hands and hips.

To better understand the difference between a swing which looks logical from the outside and a swing that performs logically from within, we will do a comparison of the swing example Hogan used in *Five Lessons*, to the standard swing model.

As seen on page 103, Hogan isolated this as a swing which spends the club's energy too soon in the downswing.
Copyright 1957 Ben Hogan.

Also shown on page 103 is an example arc, which prescribes to incorrect motion. Here, we layer that incorrect arc over the above image.

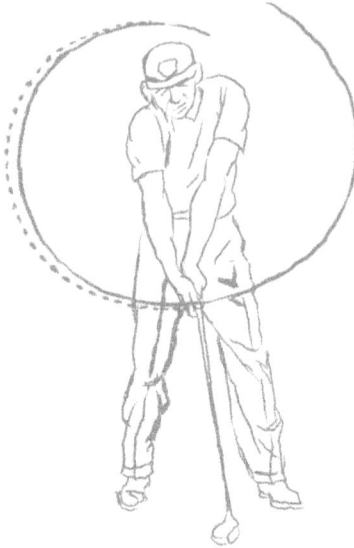

An incorrect arc superimposed on top of a golfer with early extension, as seen on page 103.

Next, let us look at a standard model golf swing. This image is created by re-situating the above golfer's body parts, into widely advisable positions.

A retooled early extension swing. Meant to correct a slice.

You'll notice the grip, the square club face and the head position, all leveraged to behind the ball. This swing type is not so different from the slicers. The arc doesn't vary much.

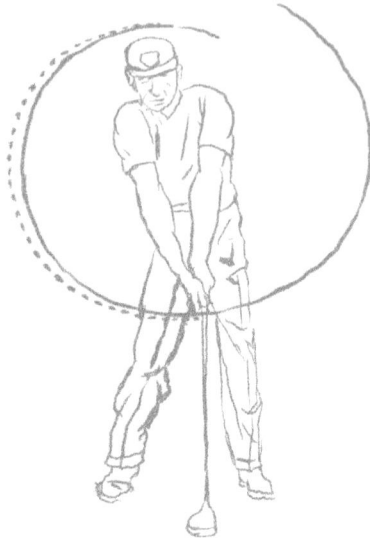

Standard model with arc. The arc is somewhat closer to the
golfer's right shoulder, and also more from the inside.

The key differences between the standard model and the
slicer's swing are found in the lead action. The lead hand and
arm has the strength to stabilize the club through impact, and
the golfer's weight moves onto the lead leg. From here, all a
golfer need to do is keep their hands passive, and launch the
ball down the line. At least that is the presumption. [3]

---

[3] I shouldn't have to point out the obvious. Creating a model of
the standard golf swing should not have been so easy. All the
further I had to look was at Ben Hogan's example of a bad
swing.

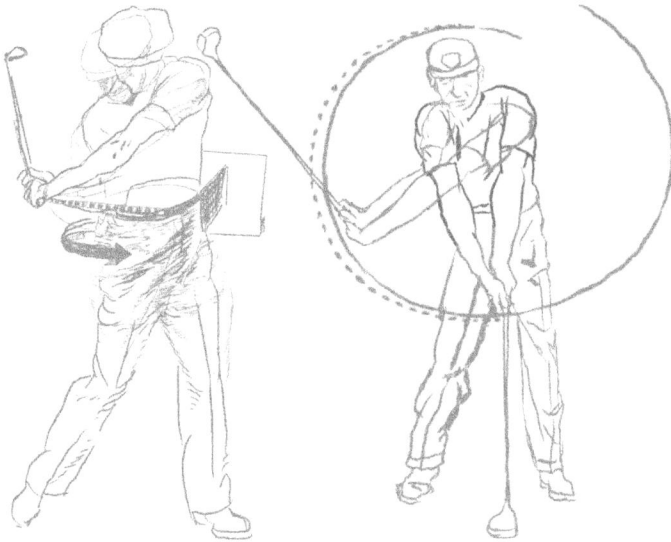

Above left, the Hogan downswing feels from pages 91 and 95, overlayed. To the right, the standard model feels, wherein the club face does not deviate from square.

Hogan welcomed the effect the turning of the hips had on the downswing. In the image, Hogan's head was most upright, and club highest up, in the thick rubber band to the wall illustration, from page 91. In the image from page 95, the club and his head had dropped.

The contrary advice, often given, is to push the arms out away from the body, in the downswing position on the right. The club face is being guided, and that is very much the feel golfers ascribe to.

There is another substantial similarity between the standard model and the slice swing. At impact, in the standard model, the golfer's hands are working the club face open, from its square position. In *Hogan How To*, we covered the club's action, as it descends into the ball. With the force of gravity alone, the club face will turn past square. Hogan recognized this, which is why he built a swing which had the club come from under the plane, *in an ascending path*. The feel for that action, and the reasoning behind it, can be found in the gravity drop exercise. If the club is not permitted to pass square, the club head will rise, to above the ball.

Hogan also cupped his wrist in the back swing. That way, the club face never need be opened through impact. Here is an exaggeration of what must be done with the club face, through impact, in the standard swing. We learned from our gravity fall exercise, in *Hogan How To* dropping the club onto the back of the ball causes the face to close past square. That action must be countered, in the standard model, the golfer must counter turn with their hands, as their hips are opening the other way. This is because the hands and hips are conjoined. As Hogan established. In a Hogan swing, the club face is allowed to square in tandem with the opening of the hips.

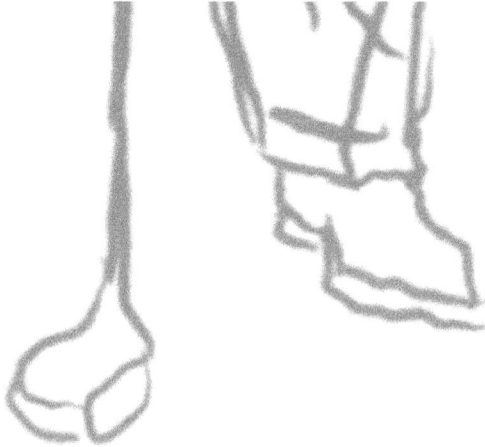

The standard swing model requires the club face to be opened
away from the turning of the hips, through impact.

Presenting an illustration of how amateurs view the swing
(and even misguided professionals) is the easiest of almost
any. Hogan already had that illustration made. You'll recall
the example from the first chapter, which showed correct and
incorrect placement of the grip through the "trail" hand?
Hogan did the same thing on pages 88 and 89. Only, since he
was protecting his secret, he didn't point out the incorrect
approach. Instead, he left that secret for pioneers to uncover. [4]

----

[4] On page 26, the correct grip placement was solid and the
incorrect grip placement was dotted.

The illustration from page 89 (top) is done of a golfer other than Hogan, from a down the line point of view. The arrows in the plane images, (below) show how golfers other than Hogan perceive golf shots. Thinking they must apply their efforts down the line. Their best attempts result in the swing from Chapter 2. A slight draw swing.

On page 88, the above image (not shown) is of an overly large pane of glass. Overly large because then it is the same size as the golfer-with-Hogan-image on the other side of the fold. Just like the example on page 26, Hogan presented us with correct and incorrect. Below the overly large image of the pane of glass is the correct motion. The motion Hogan uncovered.

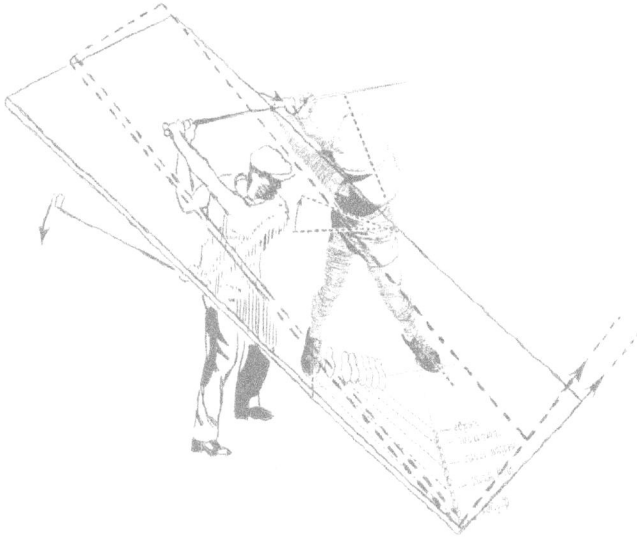

Shown here is the backswing, downswing illustration from page 88, overlayed with the composite from Chapter Two of *Hogan How 2*. This depiction was not hard to arrive at, as the geometry of the golf swing is such that our intentions and our positions align.

When we align the arc along the backswing, downswing plane, we see how very different Hogan's methods were from the standard model.

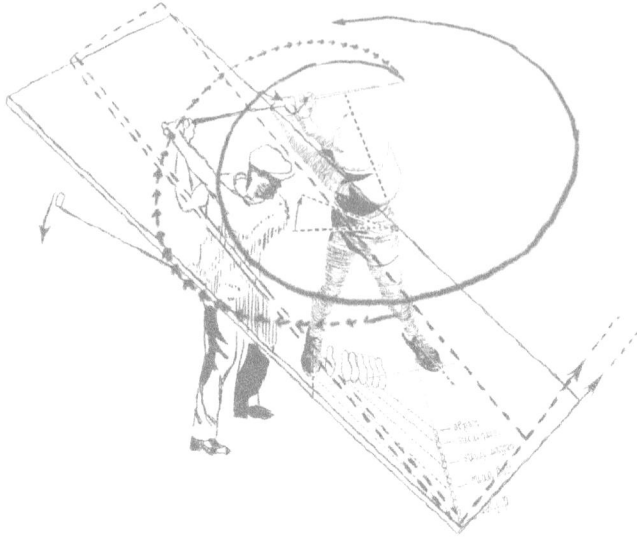

The backswing, downswing plane from page 88, the pivot from page 45, and the correct backswing, downswing arc from page 103 all align neatly.

We see in the arrows from this most recent image how Hogan opened the club face, at the top, and permitted it to stay open as the hips initiated the swing. Hogan appears to have resolved the question, "when should the hands cause the club face to be opened?" With a rudimentary answer, "certainly not at impact!"

To a logical thinker, like Hogan, the willful manipulation of the club did not make sense. He fought a hook, early in his career because he instinctively understood that the swing should be guided by the big muscles. However, the commonly shared viewpoint held that the club must be pulled down to the ball. Indeed, Sam Snead said his first move was to pull down with his left hand. Hogan came to understand how detrimental that first move was.

Pulling the club head down to the ball places emphasis on a golfer's ability to manipulate the club face through impact. First, by closing the face in the down swing, then by advancing the hands far enough leading into impact to undo the overly closed face. And furthermore, by keeping the dominant hand out of the swing long enough to prohibit the club face from turning over. Which is the thing physics is trying very, very hard to accomplish.

Admittedly, the swings we see on tour are a combination of the two examples. There are tour swings that open the club face wide in the backswing, and almost every touring professional experiences some drop of their head, early in the downswing. Ironically, the greatest golfer to immediately follow Ben Hogan pointed the club face at the sky, at the top of the backswing, and didn't let his head descend, at all. That golfer, of course, was Jack Nicklaus. Jack Nicklaus, at his prime also had two of the strongest legs the game has ever seen.

We're currently seeing a repeat of this talent. In Scottie Scheffler, with his flying right elbow, skyward club face and prominent leg action.

Reader, if you have Jack Nicklaus's strength, or Scottie Scheffler's, and profound natural ability, I trust you are reading this book for the mere joy of contemplating golf. If, on the other hand, you are like me, and so countless many others, advice on how *not to* rely on natural ability will be to your benefit.

"Reverse every natural instinct and do the opposite of what you are inclined to do, and you will probably come very close to having a perfect golf swing." Ben Hogan.

Chapter 3

Letting Go

You may recall, in the prologue of this book, a challenge I propositioned myself with. The risk, when playing golf, is losing what we have. Truly, though, that is a risk not enough golfers take. I had to ask myself, after seeing my handicap drop five shots, if I hadn't cut myself short. The next move will completely abandon the number one presumption in golf. There is an adage the vast majority of golfers have abandoned, customarily at the request of more knowledgable authorities, "keep your head down."

Indeed, that adage describes more than a physical limitation. If you've read my previous work, you may recall the lesson from modeling the swing of Annika Sörenstam. Wherein escaping the limitations of singular focus, on impact, freed my swing (and mind). The movements I am about to describe come straight from *Five Lessons* and have a comparable effect.

We all understand the importance of a good divot. That ball first axiom is the basis of every golfer's education. Indeed, as a competitor in high school, the lesson we were repeatedly given, and admonished for relinquishing, consisted of a line on the ground we were not to disturb, and a tee ahead of the ball we were to also strike.

This is what I've discovered was missing from that lesson; the golf shot. We presume good impact will result in a good shot. However, our mind disconnects from the shot, when we connect it to the ground. As Mr. Hogan said, "the ultimate judge of your swing is the flight of the ball."

Let us put that statement into perspective. The subject is not the shot, the subject is the swing, the object is the shot. We swing the club to coincide with the desired shot. We are coming to realize, through in-depth analysis of *Five Lessons*, Hogan left little unaddressed.

So, back to the conundrum I contemplated, as fall set in and my final rounds of the regular season wrapped up. Like many golfers, I stood over the ball, measuring my confidence of the lie and applying myself mentally to a construct of the shot. To me, the image was that of the ball flying through the air, at the onset. Here is a picture from *Hogan How To* which illustrates the visual.

The image from page 85, along with the target from page 99,
duplicated to indicate both ball flight and hand path.

I found myself unable to concentrate on the ball flight, and
when my concentration wasn't there the shots would go awry.
Truthfully, I had thought up some improvements to make to
my boat, and that preoccupation was costing me focus. Even
still, "golf is not a game of good shots. It's a game of bad
shots," Ben Hogan.

Perhaps I was emphasizing something that made hitting
golf shots more work than it needed to be. Now, the mind
starts to reel. Think of not trying to control the outcome of a
golf shot. Imagine reaching a point to where your golf swing

is such that you apply effort only to the action, not to your expectation.

I could see the answer in the above image. There are two bullseyes. One which necessitates effort, and another which does not. In the previous chapter, the example of the standard model golf swing ascribes to the idea of club face control. The supposition is that the best golfers have the greatest club face control. They manage, through a compendium of effort and ability, to execute exacting club face positions, at extreme speeds, for milliseconds, at impact.

Now, ask yourself how Hogan was able to hit so many fairways and greens. The man was human, after all. A greyhound bus provided us with that all-too gut-wrenching reality. We are all human. We feel the taxation of golf. For so many of us, the thought of playing more than four rounds *a year* of individual tournament golf is too much to bear. So how was another human being able to play so many, so well, even after suffering a debilitating accident? [5]

The solution is *not* less effort. Lowering our workload does little to improve our outcome. There are times, when we've all thought, the way to execute good shots is unconsciously. Only to realize unconscious action is a paradox. The harder we think about not trying, about letting ourselves slip into "the zone," the more the zone evades us.

Effort must be applied to correct action.

---

[5] Mr. Hogan and his wife, Valerie, were in a head on collision with a Greyhound bus, on February 2nd of 1949. Doctors believed Hogan probably would never walk again, much less play golf.

It's right there, in *Five Lessons*. We can plainly see where the correct action must go. This image, from the previous chapter, was configured in order of magnitude. From left to right, culminating at impact. This first, left most image is the one that helped free up my swing. (The rehearsal motion from *Hogan How To* gets us a long way down this road).

Working left to right, for to aft, we unravel the precedent for a well struck shot. The arc around the foreground swing positions highlights two key moments. The moment in line with the front foot, and at the uppermost part of the swing. Denoted by the arrow.

We've established how important that moment, in line with the lead foot, is to the golf swing. Readers of *Hogan How To* have also seen the rehearsal motion built around the perpendicular for that foot, which leads to the hip target, from earlier in this chapter. (On page 40) If we also borrow from Hogan's plane illustrations, (from page 88) we must ask ourselves why on earth was the one drawn so big?

The answer is found in the question, where is the swing going? If you're anything like I was, up to recently, you obsess over where the *ball is going.* But what if the key to success lies with the outcome of the swing? In the through swing image, from above, we see an arrow in the arc. An arrow which does not exist in the bad swing example. The bad swing example spends all its energy at the ball.

The good swing example spends it on the arrow!

The glass plane was so big because that bigness is what drove Hogan's swing. If you haven't seen videos of his ferocious through swing, seek them out. They are a beauty to behold. Here is the rub. That motion cannot be arrived at by following the shot. The golfer must let go!

The key is not to relinquish ourselves of effort, or care. Diminishing gumption does but one thing, reduce value. Instead, we must spend our effort on that which we can control.

Once we've established a trust in our swing, that it will repeatedly pass that point ahead of the front toe, we must go beyond. Beyond is not along the flight of the ball. As I have supposed for long, many years. Beyond is to where *Five Lessons* guides us. I now find that my focus turns from the line of flight, at address, to beyond the pre-established position, from the rehearsal motion.

The outcome is that of the club chasing hard and fast through impact, and up into the air, riding on the full force of my trail arm, as it releases its energy. An absence of understanding would lead us to believe we must launch the club skyward. There is a mid-point though, between impact and the top of the through swing, which must be pursued.

We know, from the image which tethers the wrist to the hips, that the hips lead the hand action. The hips must lead the way to the arrow at the top of the arc. Readers of *Hogan How To* will recall how the hip action is the best way to descend the club to the inside of the ball. In doing so, the hands remain in a neutral position. That way, the squareness of the club face is not altered by shaft lean.

Once that condition, descending the club on the ball with the hips, is arrived at, the need to monitor the squareness of the club face with feelings in the hands no longer exists. At which point, the golfer's attention must go onward. Below is the contra example, of what happens in a standard swing when the golfer gets stuck.

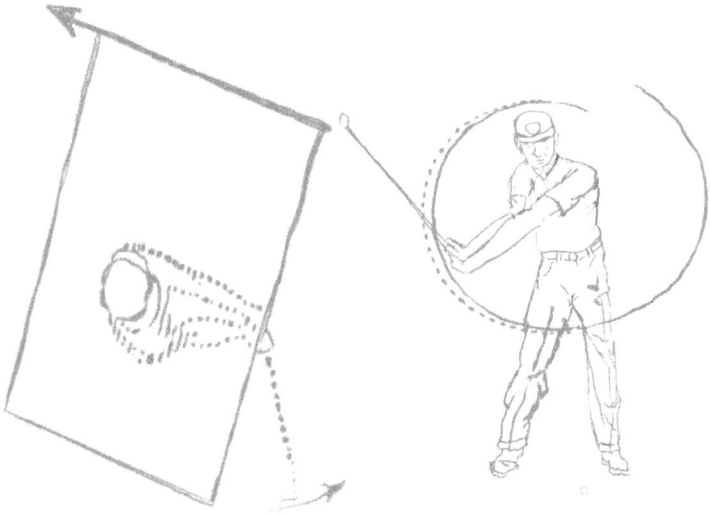

At about this moment, in the downswing, the golfer will have achieved the expectation of a square face en route to impact.
The perilous mistake is to believe good contact is certain.
That presumption will cause the hips to stall, along with the golfer's body weight. And a mishit will result.

In the Hogan swing model, assessing the squareness of the face is unnecessary. Which is why Hogan provided instruction, which gets us beyond the stuck point, beyond the ball, and through the shot.

Chapter 4

Connecting The Dots

At address, we experience the target as being to the side. Interestingly, Hogan did not emphasize the target line, in his address diagram. The target line, and emphasis on impact, are two assumptions golfers make. A golfer could well be better off were they to read Five Lessons before ever hitting a ball. That way, they would not have trepidation over straight and solid. Instead, they could apply themselves to correct motion, without anxiety.

Only at address, are we nearly parallel to the target. At impact, our body is turned open to the target, in line with the turn. One of the irrefutable things Jack Nicklaus said he learned from Hogan, about the golf swing, is that, "it should be made from the ground up."

Let us begin with the ground, work our way up to the center of the swing, then around to the finish. And see how that progression compares with the limitations of the standard model. We know that the standard model and Hogan's methods differ by the slice metric. Slicing, as I've said, is illogical. A slice results from a lack of muscle. Plain and simple. The mere act of swinging the golf club should build the muscles in the lead arm.

In Hogan's day, Spalding was the leading golf club company. This Executive iron was built in 1964 and tends toward toe weighting.

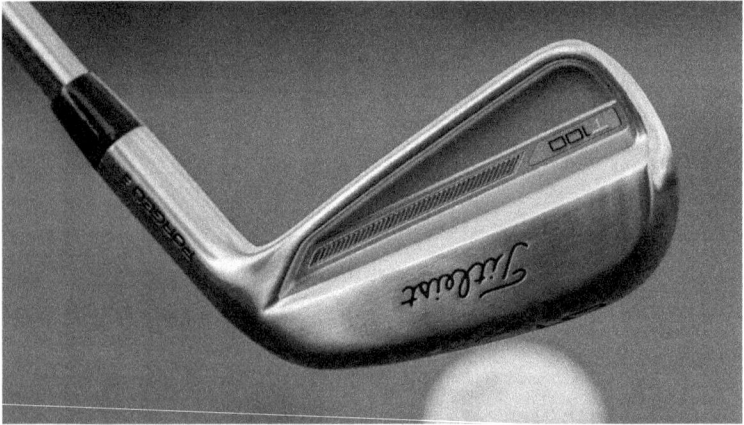

A modern Titleist iron is similarly weighted toward the toe.

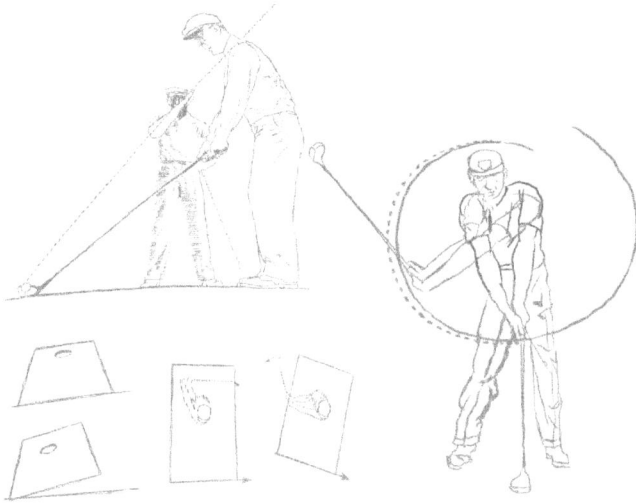

The amateur approach to an inside arc is supported by golf club construction, which favors toe weighting.

In the downswing position shown, the club face is on its way closed. The weight of the club head accelerates this closing action. As the golfer approaches impact, weighting toward the toe helps keep the club face from turning over.

Slicers spend the turning of the club face too early. They interpret the standard release as being on an axis around their dominant arm. The reliance of golfers, indeed all athletes — on their dominant arm — is why Hogan's methods are superior.

Hogan irons of today keep their weighting nearer to the heel of the club.

Weighting the club toward the heel causes the club to lead down from the top shaft first, then as the club approaches impact, it swings shut like a door. The hozel acting as a hinge. [6]

When we look at videos of Hogan, we see him aligning the ball off the heel of the club first. He undertook club manufacturing to resolve the final component of a sure swing. He had resolved the grip, ball position, stance, and action.

---

[6] Closing a narrow closet door takes less effort than closing a wide entry door. Even if they weigh the same.

The only remaining element was the configuration of the club head.

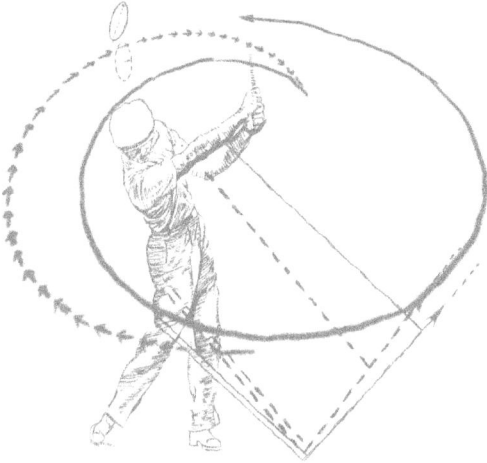

By comparison, the Hogan method puts the dominant arm in charge, firing down and through. Never halting to measure and manipulate the club face. It is an action of absolute confidence.

The down and in motion seen here revolves around the center of the swing. Note how no instruction in *Five Lessons* save for the one showing an amateur, from page 89, includes the ball? There are images of Hogan striking the ball, but they are not instructive. The Hogan method depends upon relieving a golfer of their obsession with striking the ball. [7]

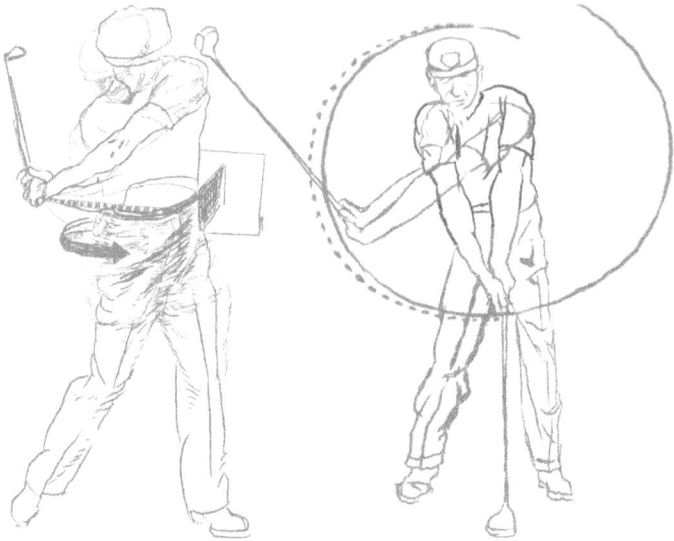

In the standard model, the trail arm must ride along. The
Hogan initiation of the hips creates the turn and fire position
above. Allowing the dominant arm room to execute.

The extraordinary benefit of training my non-dominant arm
to act as a dominant arm is understanding. Engaging an arm
with 60% strength as if it could be "three right hands," has
provided knowledge. The know-how Hogan had could not be
arrived at with natural ability alone. Not with an everyday

---

[7] Author's note: playing left-handed, with a non-dominant hand
in trail position, the challenge of engaging that arm has
perpetuated through the swing. At every juncture, the next
question is, "how to keep the left arm moving?"

golfer's natural ability. Hogan's understanding of the swing was such that a common approach could never compare.

He was kind enough not to point out how endemic the approach seen on page 89 would become. Instead, he left it to us to evaluate the comparison between page 88 and page 89. He showed us the correct motion, and then showed us the incorrect motion. The enlarged pane of glass on page 88 was drawn that way because it is almost exactly the same size as the dotted pane on page 89. We were supposed to draw comparisons between the images on page 88, which show Hogan's methods, and the flawed approach, in the images on page 89.

We are about to see how engaging the "trail" arm, to its utmost, involves abandonment of the one thing that gets in almost every golfer's way.

Pictured here is the author's 1971 Hogan Medallion 1 iron.
The heel of the club protrudes from the hozel.

Following The Hips

From *Hogan How To* "Then we perceive the flight of the ball. We perceive the flight because it will pass through the bullseye, at that height."

Query a thousand golfers and almost every one of them will answer this question in the same way. "Which is the more important target?"

Indeed, the vast majority of golfers can spend years, possibly even their whole career developing the lessons in *Hogan How To*. Some golfers will reach a point, on their way to professional level golf, when they realize the benefit of a freewheeling swing.

A very good thing happens when we acquaint ourselves with the belt buckle target. We experience the body turn first and then empower our dominant hand to feel as though it is catching the ball from the ground and hurling it through the bullseye. Credit *Hogan How To*

Hogan didn't merely say he knew a secret that would enable amateurs to play professional level golf. He said he, "had a secret that would enable.. professionals to shoot in the 50s." Any professional who has gone that low would say they were able to swing without conscious action. The ball simply went where they intended.

One of the common attributes of tour players swings is a flat lead wrist at the top of their backswing. The idea is that they have preset the impact position. Hogan advocated for cupping the lead wrist at the top of the backswing. Proponents of the flat lead wrist argue Hogan's method required timing, and theirs does not.

The opposite is actually true. In our discussion of the function of the golf swing, we compared Hogan's motion to the closing of a door, on a hinge. A flat left wrist at the top creates a secondary action, the hinge must slide along. Picture a door on a track, like a sliding door, and also on a hinge. Instead of merely opening and closing the door, the wrist must also estimate the amount of slide. The size of the door varies through the bag. With the short irons, the slide must happen sooner because the door is smaller, and the slide will quicken as it closes. With long clubs, the slide can happen later. Incorrect timing will plague clubs of a certain length, while other clubs will play fine.

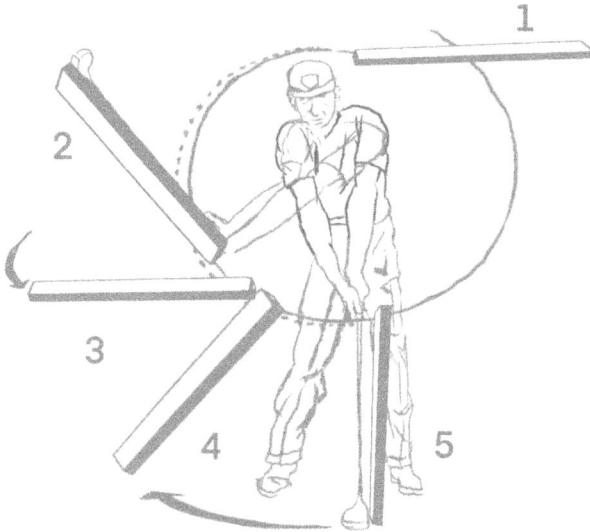

In position 1, at the top, the golfer squares the club with his arm. In position 2 it opens slightly, as the body begins its turn. In position 3 gravity takes hold and tries to shut the club face. In position 4 the club face is closing hardest, and the golfer must counter rotate the closing of the face. Using their hands, they must get the amount of counter rotation correct at position 5.

That is why the standard model instructs us to place the ball in the middle of our stance, on short irons, and vary that position through the bag. The advice is made to attempt to resolve the amount of slide the wrist will have. With short irons and wedges, the golfer is expected to advance their hands a great deal, in order to open the club face to square. Yet another variable that is difficult to reproduce.

The swings we see in instructional videos (commonly on YouTube and other social media platforms) are near carbon copies of this action. The standard model is a beta version of the slice swing. The club wants to close over and the golfer, even good golfers—even professionals—must fight the face coming into impact.

Hogan held his lag so long because he was never attempting to slide. He knew where to place the ball, in his stance, because of where he was going. His swing did not depend upon his attention being divided between the turn and the club position at impact. He needed only focus on turning in time with the closing of the face.

At one point, Tiger Woods set out to resolve a stuck position. He described excess lag and the need to "catch up" coming into the ball. We may remember the use of the word "Olay" to describe the flash hand action he relied upon. In his work with Butch Harmon, he resolved that problem. Whether Hogan's methods are an improvement on that correction is up to Tiger and Butch. [8]

In the above images, of Hogan with two bullseyes, the caption in *Hogan How To* describes his foot pointing at Ravielli. We see that description is not entirely true. The horizon line points outside his lead foot.

Let us think back to the transposed lead foot position, from this image.

---

[8] In my opinion, Hogan would have advocated for mentally continuing his release, beyond the ball. To me, and judging from the images in *Five Lessons* Hogan as well, the true nature of a stuck golf swing resounds at impact. Where too much focus completely derails the benefits of the swing.

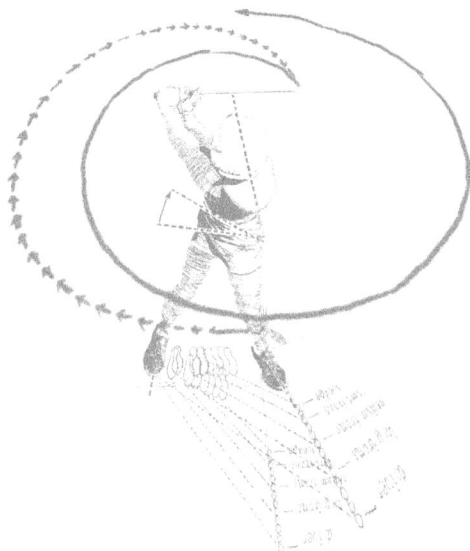

In the process of swinging the hips to the two-handed pass bullseye, the lead foot will endeavor to open and fall back.

The harder a person tries to compel this transfer, the less intrusive the squaring of the club becomes. Bryson DeChambeau hits a toe draw because he doesn't understand the merits of the cupped wrist. His weight moves correctly, but the club is on its way past shut. He has tried to embody Hogan's methods, but misinformation has led his hands astray. Hogan enjoyed a non-slide hand action. His ball position remained consistent, and his hands slid not at all.

As for the differences between short irons and woods, or mid-irons or long irons, Hogan had no dismay. He simply adjusted one foot. Golfers following the standard model must move the ball in their stance, time their slide for the club, and *lift up* at impact with the driver. It is no wonder golfers complain about never being able to get all aspects of the game correct, at once.

Hogan's stance varied through the bag, because of the relationship with the two-handed basketball pass bullseye. When we stand closer to the ball, our hips have less room to move. In his stance description, he advocated for setting up with the stance open on short irons. At first, it may feel strange to address the ball off the lead heel, with a short iron or wedge. That feeling goes away, when the two-handed basketball target factors into the stance.

Readers of *Hogan How To* will recall the turning point position. From there, the triangle created between the foot and the club face becomes smaller with smaller clubs. Hogan described the two-handed pass bullseye being between four and five yards away. Indeed, that triangle will measure between four and five yards, based on club length.

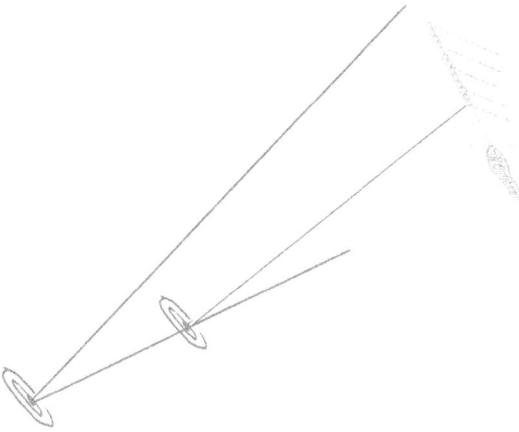

Even though the distance from the ball to the foot is not accurate, (closer to the swing a point along the shaft concept) the ratio of four to five yards holds true.

My advice to Bryson is to abandon the notion that a flat left wrist is to his benefit. Allow the door to close on its hinges alone. The body can do all the work, and body motion is so much easier to coordinate. Can you imagine his game if he combined his power with the control of a fade?

How does a swing, which comes sharply from the inside produce a fade? Because it turns hard. No slide. Just turn. Hogan built his swing around turning over the lead leg. Even though his clubs were built to shut, his swing was built to open. The further along we chase the Hogan motion, the mightier that turn must be.

Chapter 5

From The Ground UP

Every other image in this book is derived from ones with dotted lines. Of the 61 illustrations in *Five Lessons*, 23 have dotted lines. *Five Lessons* is so full of information, major breakthroughs can be found in just about a third of the content.

This illustration depicts the action which leads to one of Mr. Hogan's most peculiar pieces of advice. He once said something to the effect of, "when you get it right, you can feel it in the muscle next to your left nut."

As peculiar as that piece of advice sounds, it gives a clear indicator. Golfers will experience that sensation when they execute the above motion. Let's delve deeper into the image.

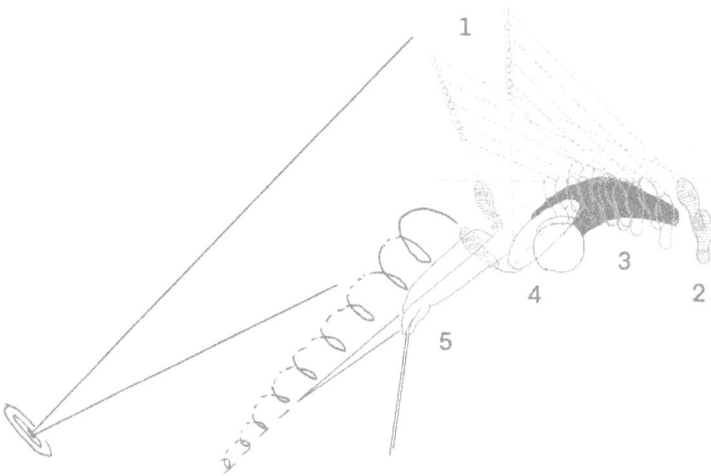

1. The ground angles, established at setup, the basketball pass bullseye is at the end of a triangle created by the lead foot and the line extending through that foot, to the club head, (in the turning point position from *Hogan How To*). It is easy to establish this target, at

address, by simply looking down the perpendicular from the front foot four or five yards.

2. The way the feet move in the golf swing doesn't just look good. Seen in the back foot is the cause for the golfer to finish on their toe. In the front foot we see how the weight must turn away, and fall back from, the ball.

3. The shaded segment depicts the right knee movement, in the downswing. In Jody Vasquez's book *Afternoons With Mr. Hogan,* he described a piece of advice Mr. Hogan gave. He said the advice was along the lines of, "drive your right knee at the ball." That never really made sense. We know driving the right knee at the ball creates some bad effects. My right-handed swing suffered those effects. Then I realized, the true intent of the advice was to drive the right knee toward the bottom of the swing. We also know the bottom of the swing as its turning point.

4. You may say, "the turn must happen well before the club gets to that point." And you are correct. Our intentions must always precede the motions of the swing. That is how we avoid getting stuck, as so many practitioners of the standard model often do. Which is why the hips open as far as the weight shift over the front foot. Seldom will a golfer generate the torque to actually move their front foot to that new position. However, the hips should reposition the body weight to reflect its new stance.

5. The twisting of the arms in this drawing is exaggerated, to illustrate the feeling. Just as Hogan said, the target for the basketball pass is at about the height of the belt buckle. Attempt to make the pass motion to a target at that height, in line with the turned hips, and you will find an impossibility that puts your swing in the best positions. Your arms simply cannot throw that low. Instead, the body forces the arms upward, to the arrow in the arc image.

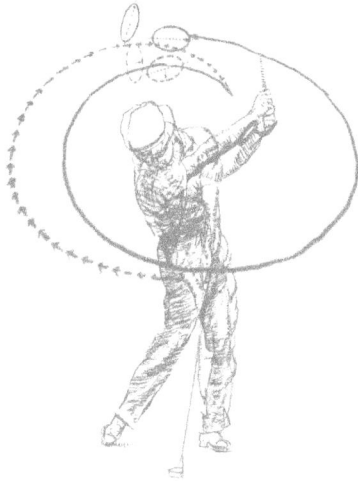

The image of the arc, from page 103, superimposed over
impact position and through swing position, from page 122
demonstrates the starting point of the arc, at the swing's
center, and the lifting of the arms. Which is caused by the
impedance of the body.

Attempt this motion. Do so using Hogan's 9-3 drill, from
pages 82 and 83. Concentrate not on an imaginary ball.
Instead, think only of the motions of the body. Note how
attempting to turn your arms over, as shown in the "from the
ground up" image, causes your wrist to want to cup (in the
backswing), then roll in the through swing. [9]

---

[9] The first portion in the 9-3 drill gives a powerful clue to the
symmetry of the golf swing. Note how the shading does not
exist between the left and right halves of the body? The

Three positions of the 9-3 drill, from pages 106 & 107, depicting the cupping of the lead wrist, in the back swing, the rolling motion approaching impact, and the hip, arm synchronization in the through swing.

Next, attempt to keep your wrist flat in the backswing, as prescribed by the standard model. Note how attempting to turn through the shot now causes your body to form this shape:

---

transfer, from one side to the other, is a key component of a great golf swing.

Even professional golfers are doing opposite things with their hands and bodies. The body wants to turn. If you allow your hands to move with the turn, they will create the shape Hogan outlined, in the Life magazine article. His cupping of the wrist that so many golf instructors rail against, is actually the natural way to tie the action of the hands to the turning of the body.

Epilogue

The subject of ambidextrousness needs attention. Hogan denied being left-handed. A rumor he attributed to his use of a left-handed five iron when he was new to caddying. Were he left-handed, his instruction would be easy to dismiss. I've found greater understanding from playing the game from my non-dominant side. And it would be easy to say he had done the same.

How much of standard instruction is intent on eliminating difficulty with the non-dominant lead arm? The function I call a slide, where the lead arm is put into position early in the downswing and meant to sustain that position, appears to be an attempt to alleviate complex lead hand function.

The problem, as I see it, is the slide motion also eliminates the dominant hand from the swing. I attribute my injuries to attempting to combine the two methods. In 2007, I needed to hit a low drive into a thirty mile per hour wind. I did so by radically bowing my lead wrist, coming into impact.

(As I've stated about the slide, it can wait longer with long clubs, but must happen early with short ones. A variable which makes the standard method difficult to repeat, through the bag).

It would be dismissive to say this one swing did all the damage. When I was a teen golfer, I would practice on a rug on concrete, throughout the winter. Not being an easily satisfied person. I would swing every bit as hard on that rug as I would on grass. I could feel that ligament ache. Each time it would, I would lay off my practice. So, it was a stressed ligament.

The sensation I felt that day, was of a bomb exploding in my wrist. I had been working out Hogan's Angle for nearly a decade. Except, unlike the earliest versions, I was trying not to do the Sörenstam peek. As a result, there was a great deal of tension, between a lead wrist which was sliding and a (forceful) dominant hand which was releasing. The drive did as I intended. It flew low, almost parallel to the ground, and rolled out, to within a tiny punch shot from the green. However, my left wrist was no more.

That was the last time I made that shape with my lead hand and arm. Until, taking the game up left-handed. Like many serious golfers, I'd dabbled with left-handed shots. But never really thought I could play the game well from that side. My right arm is so strong, I hardly needed my left, though. Except, a strictly lead arm swing has its detriments.

The slide works well on the range. Before developing Hogan's Angle, with the Sörenstam peek, I hit the ball so well on the range an onlooker would have figured me for a scratch golfer. Indeed, the pro would never let me play with all my strokes in tournaments. He saw how I could hit the ball. On the practice tee.

A slide doesn't work well from uneven lies though, or through the bag. Anyone who has seen Eldrick Tiger Woods talk about hitting shots from uneven lies knows that he attributes his excellence to feels in his right hand. When I got serious about playing left-handed, I found myself back in the early stages of the game. Using the slide to avoid the slice, and developing a practice tee swing. The kind that works well in practice, then disappoints in play. But then, distance was the only really metric. As so is often the case.

Boy, would I ever helicopter that golf club. My shot was never a draw, and only did I hook the ball when my brain took over (as frequently is the case with the slide), and said, "don't push it!" Instead, the shot has always been a fade. Videos of my swing, up to rebuilding from the center two years ago, demonstrate just how quick wristed my lead hand motion was.

Golfers with overly strong lead hand grips will make that helicopter action. The great man, Arnold Palmer, had a profound helicopter finish. Jim Thorpe followed, and commentator Paul Azinger, both with very strong lead hand grips, would helicopter the club through the finish. David Duval is a good example of how strong lead hand motion can lead a person to need to peek through the swing. Turning your head towards the target alleviates pressure, created by an early slide. It keeps the body moving, so the slide doesn't come to an abrupt halt.

I started teaching myself to do athletic things left-handed, at the age of 20. Starting with big balls, by shooting baskets, and then moving on to football. In football, I throw too hard with my right hand, for close passes, but no further than 20–25 yards with my left. So, if I actually worked at it, I could be a good quarterback, for a non-existent Geritol league.

The standard approach solved my slice, when I took up the game at fourteen and got me to an eleven handicap, left-handed. I improved right-handed by getting beyond the standard approach. (By standard I am referring to the divot focused, minimized trail hand, maximally flat lead-wrist action the vast majority of instruction revolves around).

Getting better at golf, from both sides, has meant getting beyond impact. Now, thanks to Ben Hogan, I'm able to do so without relying on magical thinking. That was the hardest part of the Sörenstam peek. I couldn't understand why it worked. Hogan's methods make sense. Indeed, the standard model makes sense, rudimentarily. It's great for getting people to play the game, without too much embarrassment. [10]

When I used the peek to play good golf, I relied on it to show up, during the swing. Unlike the peek move, the rehearsal motion I developed for *Hogan How To* presets a good shot. Unlike the standard model, the Hogan methods lay out a holistic approach. The rehearsal motion has made it possible to play practice tee golf, on the golf course.

Taking the swing this next step, completely getting beyond impact—over the object, the ball, and into the aspects of the swing I control—has me feeling more confident in my golf game than ever. When I visualized golf shots leading into last season, I foresaw an electric explosion. Capabilities my mind could not detail. That explosion came to fruition, as the rehearsal motion came together.

Now, when I visualize golf shots, I see myself turn. As demonstrated in the "from the ground up" illustration in the

---

[10] Foot dominance, in my opinion, is a greater factor in a golfer's best side of the ball to play from, than hand dominance. In board sports, almost all of us have a preferred front foot. Mine is right foot forward. If we stand on the corresponding side of the ball we will feel more comfortable turning through the shot. That is why playing left-handed, goofy footed (right foot forward) is more comfortable for me.

previous chapter. And, without undue effort, absent constraints over the direction of the ball. Only with the feeling of my momentum as it unfurls. I see the golf ball fly, from a partially open club face, with a slight fade, to the target.

My body is on its way down the right field line, and the ball takes off over second base, only to curve ever so slightly and carry well beyond the center fielder. Who must turn slightly to his right, to see the ball leave the stadium.

I feel this swing in my buttocks, and the muscles in my legs. Specifically, in that muscle inside the lead thigh. The one Hogan bluntly referred to as, "next to the left nut." Only, for me, it's next to the other one. I feel it before it happens, in rehearsal, which is so much more pronounced than the tiny waggle Hogan used. Nonetheless, that feeling he described, of sensing the shot as if it had already come off, is the feeling I'm having.

I feel it in the target I set my feet to, and in the target my turn will transfer my weight to. I feel it in the certainty the ball will start precisely where it was and end where it is meant to go. Furthermore, I feel it in the space between my backside and my finish. At address, at impact, and in the outcome.

I feel it in the way my left hand moves through impact, to the finish, not with a jarring sensation of club and ball, and anxious anticipation. Rather, with the all-too-free feeling of extending, along with the club, to the arrow at the end of the arc.

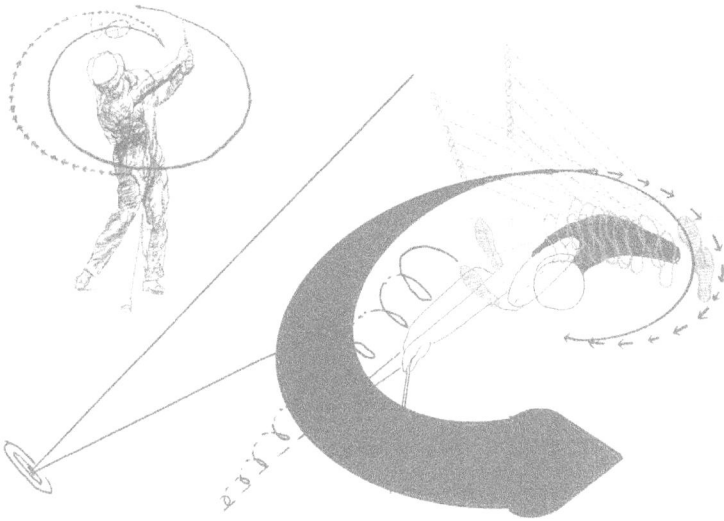

Hogan contact and through swing images from page 122, of *Five Lessons* overlayed with the correct swing arc, from page 103. Along side "from the ground up"

And, because we're talking about my feels. Here is the left-handed version.

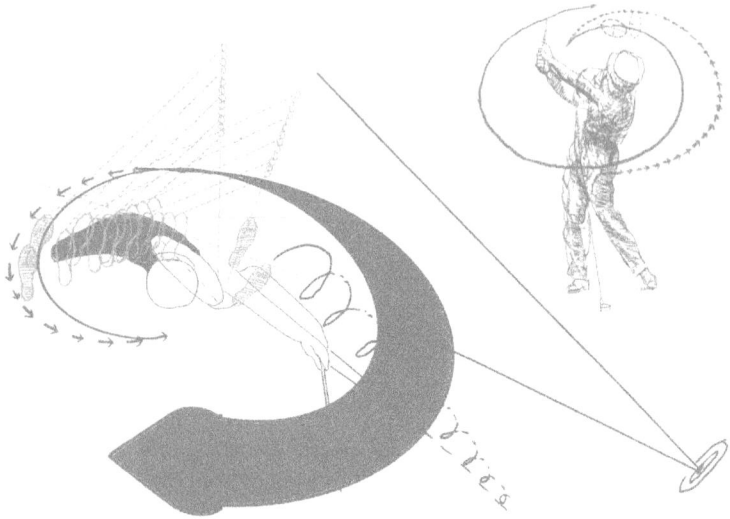

This feeling of release. Of relinquishing one's self of the ball, and the flight of the ball. Of being ahead of the outcome. It is the exhalation my first book *Hogan's Angle: From Integration to Exaltation* was meant to arrive at. Alas, it was published only months before my wrist completely gave out, and I became unable to even take the club back. These are the followups that were meant to be.

My greatest regret, over that lost time, is on behalf of the golfers who may have benefited from further work, on the subject. Who, like myself, struggled to assimilate the standard model into their personal beliefs.

I dedicate this final chapter to my brother, Harley. Who was a much greater artist than I. It was his encouragement, and chiding, that made me further my abilities. To a point to where I could reliably illustrate a concept. In the hope that golfers may be inspired.

Addendum

More additional tidbits

In *Hogan How To,* I introduced the rule of thumb. In the time since, I've puzzled over visualizations that will aid with playing in the wind. I live in Central Montana, where wind is a prevailing factor. The difference between believing I may shoot in the 60s and believing I'll be happy to shoot my handicap can be summarized with one word, "wind." And I'm not talking about Herbert Warren Wind, some winds aid, and some do not. The ones that do not are far more prolific, in this part of the country.

We see tour players raise their shaft to their eye line, to align the ball with the target. Ever noticed how they don't always close an eye? If we keep both eyes open while holding the club shaft in front of us, we see two shafts. If the shaft is a consistent distance from our eyes, something interesting happens. We measure a margin.

I call this the rule of thumb because the same exercise can be done with a thumbs up. With our arm outstretched, we know we are repeating the exact distance the thumb is from our eyes. (We look foolish doing this, though.)

However, by holding the shaft up at the same distance from our eyes as our outstretched thumb, we measure a width of approximately eight percent. I.e., if we look through our shaft, at arm's length, to an object 100 yards (ca. 91 meters) away the two shafts will appear to be approximately eight yards apart.

Similarly, if we look down the fairway, over a tee shot, we will see shafts at 16 yards (ca. 15 meters) apart at 200 yards (ca. 183 meters) and 20 yards (ca. 18 meters) a part at 250 yards (ca. 229 meters).

We can use this to set markers on either side of the shot. Eight percent represents professional level shotmaking. We then know how much variance we have to hit a professional level shot. Hitting the ball the right yardage is the only thing that remains.

This trick is especially helpful when playing a new course. We don't know how far away the landing zone is, which can make us uncomfortable. By setting our markers, we establish a reasonable zone width. Which should make us more comfortable with the shot.

In addition to measuring margins, we can also visualize the effect of wind.

By first imagining our trajectory window between the two golf clubs, and getting used to the height we hit each club.

Then we can envision the effect the wind will have on the decent of the ball.

Into a head wind, quartering from the left, the decent will
have the sensation of coming toward us.

A tail wind will push the ball, to beyond its intended
destination.

The hardest thing about the wind isn't so much the movement
of the ball, as it is the ability to foresee its effects. In this way,
a person can use a repeatable metric to measure the pending
effects. With practice, this method will enable golfers to hit
shots with confidence. Which, as every prairie dweller well
knows, is the key to good wind play.

Prior works

This drawing, completed in 2011, established Hogan's Angle
as intimated from ground level.

The progression, from the ground, to the center of the swing, to the top of the through swing is the culmination of *Hogan How Two*. The following is the original thesis, *Hogan's Angle* ©2006

Hogan's Angle

by Keern Haslem

Special note to the reader

There are no pictures in this book, although there are detailed instructions. This is done purposefully. Please act out the instructions as you read them. You make the pictures. If I put them in the book they would be from my point of view anyway. By acting them out you get the most out of the instruction.

Also, act out every piece of instruction on Hogan's Angle.

◘ 1 Hogan's Angle

15/50

Chapter 1

Two questions; what is Hogan's Angle? And why haven't I heard of it before?

I'm standing before you now. Here is my hand, shake it. Nice to meet you. Don't let go. Take a good look at your arm. In what direction is it pointing?

How about an autograph? Not mine, yours. Go ahead, sign the book. Stop, are you holding a pencil or pen, are you signing the book? That could be worth a lot some day.

You're probably not driving but if you were what position would you be in? 10 and 2? Excellent, but this isn't drivers ed. Go ahead, drive, your on your way to work, or school. Get comfortable, relax. There you go.

Which hand is on the wheel? Is it your dominant hand? If not, put it up there. That's good, now tilt your seat back, go ahead it'll be cozy. Now that you're all stretched out where is your arm pointing?

Flash back to the handshake. I'm in front of you. Now, what does it take to make you mad? Whatever it is, I just did it. Go ahead, hit me.

There you go, how'd that feel. Try it again, this time in slow motion. Now, just after you've connected, pause. You're arm should be outstretched. Is it, good. Where is it pointing?

Play basketball? Take a shot, go ahead

◘ 2 Hogan's Angle

knock one down. Notice the angle of your arm after release? How about pool? Let one go, now take a look at your arm. The ball is gone, your aim on the pool cue no longer matters, yet there it is again. How about a pitch, underhand, overhand 'no matter. Let it loose and there you go, there's that angle again.

Not big into sports, no problem, have a snack. Take a bite, you'll like it. Pause at your mouth, now, extend your arm. Don't pivot at the shoulder, just stick it out straight. Huh, there must be something to this.

The scientific term probably isn't Hogan's Angle. There may not even be one, but to answer the second question. You haven't heard of Hogan's Angle because Mr. Hogan was a golfer and people think that golf is a game of hitting targets which are to the side.

What do you think? Ever considered what goes through your mind when you're standing over the ball? I'll bet it wasn't Hogan's Angle. I'll also bet it wasn't the kind of thoughts you have when you're driving to work, or school, or your home club.

Fact is, you've probably always assumed that striking the ball well required a prodigious amount of focus. Certainly, the ease you experience when driving your car could be in no way similar to swinging a golf club?

What if I told you it is? Consider what it's like to drive somewhere. Pretty easy right, follow the rules of the road, be mindful of your path and make the necessary choices. Could playing a golf course really be similar?

You tell me, after all, I can't make that decision for you. This much I can tell you, human beings were meant to play golf. The difficulty with which you have become accustomed

◻ 3 Hogan's Angle

is a facade.

People have been getting themselves and objects places for a long time. We've been hitting targets ever since they presented themselves. Doing so isn't much of a struggle, it just takes application.

Think of the last time you accomplished something. Was the task where it belongs? Right in front of you?

Golf can be that task. Don't believe me? You will, just give it a shot. Oh yea and if you haven't already realized it, your going to have to suspend disbelief.

That shouldn't be to hard, right? Every great thing you've ever done involved suspension of disbelief. Your spouse, your grades, your proudest accomplishment. You name it, at one point you doubted that you would gain that wonderful thing. Well, guess what, now it's yours. And do you know what you had to do to get it?

That's right, you had to suspend disbelief. I didn't meet and marry my wife just because, we didn't have two beautiful children like it was nothing. Before those things could happen, before every step in life can be taken disbelief must be suspended.

People who fail to do that, those who live in disbelief may have things happen. They may get married and have kids, as I have. But does their life happen or does life happen to them?

You may achieve an occasional mammoth drive. It's an unfortunate condition of reality. Sometimes awful swings produce great results.

Is your swing really awful? I know mine was, for ten years I labored to refine a swing that was built on flawed principles. Why do I

◘ 4 Hogan's Angle

say flawed? Because it's true. "Take your
instincts, do almost the exact opposite. Now you
have a near perfect swing." Ben Hogan.

We think that our experiences are new. We
somehow believe that we cause all things to
become. Maybe I'm generalizing, maybe, but I
don't think so. Golfers of all kind suppose
that, somehow they must create good golf shots.

As if the shot wasn't already there? As
if the course weren't laid out before you? We're
an arrogant species. But even our arrogance
doesn't preclude the fact that we were made to
play golf.

Hogan's Angle? It applies, believe you
me, we're talking good stuff. How good? Hogan
good.

◘ 5 Hogan's Angle

91

Chapter 2
The Dominant Arm

Ever wonder why a right handed swing is called a right handed swing? We're told to swing the club with our left hand. The right only complicates things. It's there for guidance, and leverage. The right hand connects the right side to the club and the right side is a good source of power.

Blah blah blah, we're right or left handed golfers because our dominant hand is the hand that releases best. Throw something, now do so with the other hand. Ta da, better release with the dominant hand, huh?

Now rear back like you're going to throw something real hard. Notice how your shoulders turn. Also, take a look at the position of your hand. Look anything like the top of a good golf swing?

If your standing up you probably have one foot in front of the other. To simulate another aspect of the golf swing pull that foot back, square with the other. Now, you should have your feet about shoulder width apart, your dominant hand behind you, shoulders turned and your head facing forward.

I'll bet that you couldn't maintain that position throughout the previous paragraph. Fact

◻ 6 Hogan's Angle

is you were in one coiled position. The
resistance between your hips and shoulders would
be too much to bare for long.

That resistance creates club head speed.
In the conventional golf swing attaining a good
shoulder turn takes practice and application. On
Hogan's Angle it happens naturally. As you
realized there is a great deal more coil when
your feet are square versus staggered for a
throw.

From the square position go through the
throwing motion slowly. First your hips will
start forward, followed by your shoulders, then
your upper arm, finally your lower and lastly
your wrist. That very sequence is precisely what
golfers work very hard to achieve. On Hogan's
Angle it happens naturally.

◘ 7 Hogan's Angle

Chapter 3
The Lead Arm

In Hogan's time the Frisbee hadn't been invented so, when he attempted to describe the motion of the through swing he didn't have a good comparison for the lead arm. From the square position with your lead arm, left for righties, right for lefties, pretend to throw a Frisbee.

Your elbow will bend going back, your palm will face the ground and as you come through to release and your elbow will straighten, your wrist will lead and your hand will roll to a palm up position. If you continue on through your arm will come to a halt behind your head hand raised. In grade school the teacher asked this hand up position of you when you had a question.

Do that Frisbee throw motion a few more times, only at the ball, if there were one. Notice how your wrist leads and your arm extends. This motion is called supination. Hogan used that term and, to an extent, popularized it.

Leading the golf club is almost exactly the same, the only difference is, you let the Frisbee go.

You've experienced the lead hand in its motion and the release hand in its. Now lets

◻ 8 Hogan's Angle

take a look at the two of them in combination.

Bend your knees and hips, athletically. As if you're about to return a serve in volleyball or tennis, or field a grounder. Re assume the release hand position at the top of your back swing. You're ready to make a throw. Now, direct your eyes to the ball.

Now, reach back with your lead hand. Can you reach your release hand? Probably not, if you can you weren't wound up very well. In the process of reaching two things are going to happen, your lead arm will straighten and your release arm will have to come closer to your body, once the two of them are joined you've got a straight lead arm and a release arm that's in a set position.

The straight lead arm has been thought of as an act of its own, as you can see it actually straightens to accommodate the dominant release arm.

Swing through to the finish, the lead arm leads. The release arm releases. The two throwing motions, the Frisbee with the lead arm and the standard throw with the release arm combine to create a unified motion.

Now, go on through the ball to the finish. Your release hand has released your lead hand still leads, your eventual position is the hands up position of an eager pupil, except your release hand is now connected. In the same way that your lead hand demanded that your release hand come closer to your body at the top of your back swing your lead hand must draw closer at the finish.

Rehearse each of those motions separately, the release hand making a throwing motion at the ball first. It extends behind your

◘ 9 Hogan's Angle

head, draws your shoulders open and your body snaps to life in the hips, shoulders, upper arm, lower arm, wrist sequence. Then the arm basically goes limp.

In contrast the lead arm is very relaxed in the back swing, then going through it extends, rolls to a release and remains well extended through to a halt. Once you combine those two motions your body and arms create a compact efficient swing that fires through to a full finish. The important thing is accommodating the desires of both arms. Extend to the satisfaction of the release arm in the back swing and also extend in the through swing to permit the lead arm as full a slash as possible.

◘ 10 Hogan's Angle

Chapter 4
On Hogan's Angle and The Lead Arm

You may have noticed that the lead arm does not attempt to throw along Hogan's Angle, as the release arm does. It prefers an angle which is left of that. This angle is important, as Hogan's Angle comes naturally to the dominant arm and overt domination will prohibit you from hitting a full range of shots.

Drawing the ball requires a good release. The release hand is more than happy to accommodate. Fading the ball requires a fuller through swing, the release has to be outpaced by the lead hand. Permit the lead hand an angle of its own and the beautiful cut shots which Hogan personified will be yours.

◘ 11 Hogan's Angle

Chapter 5
The Secret Hogan Searched For

The putter was not Hogan's demise so much as it was his undoing. With the putter Hogan could not achieve the simple purity that he enjoyed from tee to green. Unfortunately the satisfaction he yearned for was only eight inches away.

The lead and release made Hogan's swing work. He needed the two hands to combine in such a way that repeating his swing was automatic. With the putter there is no lead because the lead arm is bent. There is no real release either, just a dead handed motion.

Hogan tried to attain a release by building putters that were heel weighted but even then the "lead" evaded him.

Simply by moving the ball outside the left foot, toward the hole, the left arm is put in a position to lead and the right to release. After all, as Hogan said himself, the arms don't straighten until after impact.

With the putter a false impact must be created. Moving the ball about eight inches toward the hole does that. The lead and release, straight arms and a full extension/release are accomplished.

Hogan was correct with his putter

weighting. The club should be heel waited,
however it should also be toe shafted. That way,
upon release the face retreats instead of
bypassing the shaft. With a toe shafted putter
Hogan could have employed a full release.

If Hogan had read this chapter in 1946 or
thereabouts I believe he would have won as many
as double the majors he did.

The Conventional Dilemma

The hardest thing about a conventional
swing is diagnosing your misses. If, in the
process of attempting to hit a golf shot your
focus is placed on an object that is separate
from your view, that element of focus becomes an
intangible. Which makes it impossible to
ascertain the true cause of a miss, or for that
matter, a quality shot.

Consider a 150 yard shot. While in the
address position you assert your will on the
target. Place a great deal of focus on hitting
the ball there. You swing; and the ball misses
seven yards to the right.

The question is, how much of that miss
was due to your concentration? There are a
number of possibilities. Your equipment could be
ill fitted, your grip, alignment, or ball
position could be off. All sorts of things could
be wrong with your swing. It's conceivable that
three yards of the miss were due to poor
mechanics, three yards were due to an ill fitted
club and only a one yard variance was caused by
your swing. Assuming that your concentration was
perfect.

If on the following hole you face a
similar shot what will you do? Will you change
something, will you try to do the same thing you

◘ 13 Hogan's Angle

did on the previous miss? What if you get distracted and concentrate less. Only then, you hit it close.

Uh oh, you just created a situation. By concentrating less you hit the ball closer, therefore the previous miss must have been caused by poor concentration, or overexertion. But, no matter how hard you try to recreate the level of concentration that resulted in an ideal shot you continually fail.

The actual cause of the terrific shot could have been as trivial as a slope. The ball may simply have been an inch above your feet, but you were too busy concentrating on the target to notice.

Most misses are easily diagnosable, if the swing is built on the right premise. If the swing is engineered around hitting the target innumerable intangibles surface. Sometimes our will overrides our faults and we succeed. When this happens we get the false sense that our game is better than it actually is.

Pronation

In the 90's an article in Golf Digest described Hogan's Secret as a pronation or cupping of the left wrist at the top of the back swing. Hogan didn't write about that motion in "Five Lessons; The Modern Fundamentals of Golf" but he admits that he pronated in virtually every swing. Since the cupped wrist has been given a great deal of accord let's consider it for a moment.

When rearing back to really chuck a Frisbee your wrist will cock. It puts itself in a cupped position automatically, to extend your range of motion no doubt. Pronation was the lead

hands way of asserting itself at the top of
Hogan's back swing.
        Also, there is no reason for the club
face to point at the sky or the same direction
as the back of your lead arm, as conventional
swing enthusiasts would have you believe. On
Hogan's angle the target isn't to the side, the
only time the club face must be square is at
impact.
        The same is true of a pitcher in
baseball. Only at release must the ball be
heading the right direction.
        The difference between a golfer and a
pitcher is distance, for one, and attachment for
another. A pitcher throws 60 plus feet, a
golfer's hands are about three feet from the
ball. A pitcher lets go of the ball, a golfer
holds onto the club. If a pitcher can hit a mitt
consistently shouldn't golfers be able to hit
the ball well just about all the time.
        Notice how repeatable the unified lead
and release motion is? With such a repeatable
motion at your disposal only fundamentals are
going to really matter.

Hogan's Contribution

        Hogan did the two most critical things he
could. He built clubs for people to play his way
and he defined the fundamentals in exacting
detail.
        His club manufacturing company started
producing irons in 1953. Hogan irons were the
most important addition that a practicer of
Hogan's Angle could make. They were uniquely
suited to Hoganesque players. As Hogan has had
no true followers the iron market has been
dominated by offset clubs that are too upright.

◘ 15 Hogan's Angle

Although "Five Lessons: the Modern Fundamentals of Golf" is the best selling book on golf and read by virtually every tour player few, if any implement his lessons exactly.

The missing ingredient, Hogan's secret, is Hogan's Angle. With it, all things Hogan become masterfully clear.

◘ 16 Hogan's Angle

HOGAN'S ANGLE

"There is no similarity between golf and putting; they are two different games, one played in the air, and the other on the ground." Ben Hogan.

In my experience retooling my right-handed putters to fit my left-handed game, I've modified three extremely well. They place the hands at a comfortable lie angle, and provide the added benefit of aligning the shaft with the face, for correct shaft angle. Imagine bending a right-handed putter, to be used left-handed. It becomes toe-shafted.

To expand on Ben Hogan's quote, I've found a putter grip which cradles the grip between two fingers, (in both hands) like a drummer's drum stick, works very well.

Indeed, the act of making putting as different from hitting golf shots as possible has made me the best putter I've ever been.

About the author

K. Zachary Haslem "Keern" lives alternately in Montana and Nevada. He also writes stage plays, screen plays and directs television and film. For fun, he sails his beloved self-made proa, Huck Luna, (a pacific island outrigger canoe) every chance he gets. His favorite voyage being the wild stretch of the mighty Missouri River. He owes his willingness to publicize what would otherwise be a private, pleasurable outlet, his work in golf, to having found a suitable pastime. Working on and sailing his boat.

Bibliography

Hogan, Ben. Ben Hogan's Five Lessons. Simon and Schuster, 1957.

Vasquez, Jody. Afternoons with Mr. Hogan. Gotham Books, 2014.

"T-Series T100: The Modern Tour Iron." Titleist, www.titleist.com/golf-clubs/irons/t100-2023. Accessed 2 Jan. 2026.

"Irons." Irons - Ben Hogan Golf, www.benhogangolf.com/irons/. Accessed 2 Jan. 2026.

Schjolberg, Erik, et al. "Spalding Irons by Year." Swing Yard, 20 Nov. 2025, swingyard.com/spalding-irons-by-year/.

Ben Hogan Quotes - Brainyquote, www.brainyquote.com/authors/ben-hogan-quotes. Accessed 6 Jan. 2026.